MY CHRISTMAS
A PHOTOLOG BOOK

Created by Kathy Faggella and Janet Horowitz

Illustrated by Steve Jenkins

Stewart, Tabori & Chang
New York

Christmas is a magical time of year! It is probably a time that you think and dream about and plan for long before the big day, December 25th, occurs. It is also a time that you recall over and over again after the holiday has passed. Wouldn't it be fun to keep all your lists, ideas, and memories about Christmas together? Wouldn't it be great if you could keep photos of the many things you do in preparing for Christmas and during the Christmas season?

You can! Here is the opportunity for you to have even more fun with Christmas this year. With this book, a camera, film, and your own thoughts, you can capture your Christmas holiday as you see it and experience it. But best of all, you can be the photographer, reporter, and writer of your own PhotoLog book about a Christmastime that you will long remember.

Uses for your **My Christmas** book:

• Use **My Christmas** as a place to keep your personal, important thoughts and opinions about the holiday.

• Use **My Christmas** as a place to organize your preparations for Christmas.

• Use **My Christmas** for suggestions of fun things to do while getting ready for the holiday, during the celebrations, and for the rest of your vacation.

• Use the completed **My Christmas** as a gift to send to a close family member or friend who couldn't join you for your celebration this year.

• Use **My Christmas** as a record of this year's Christmas to compare with other Christmas times in your life.

• Use **My Christmas** as a treasured memory book to help you remember this special time with your family and friends.

Some hints to help you complete your book:

1. Take photos.

Be prepared to take photos of your whole Christmas celebration, from the earliest preparations until the last decoration is put away. Use the photo captions to help guide your picture taking. Try and take candid as well as posed photos. You can take all the photos yourself, or ask someone to take a few so that you can be in them. One roll of 24-print film will be enough for this book.

2. Observe your special way of celebrating Christmas.

You can get a lot of the information for this book by observing your special way of celebrating Christmas and by jotting down your thoughts as they occur to you, so that you won't forget them. To learn more you might want to talk things over with your family.

3. Fill in this book.

When your pictures are ready, decide which ones best fit the photo captions and pages of this book. Complete the fill-ins at any time, by yourself or with other people. Follow the order in this book, or skip around, whatever makes you feel comfortable. You do not have to fill in everything. And remember, have fun!

Christmas is:

- ☐ giving gifts
- ☐ visiting family and friends
- ☐ getting gifts
- ☐ having visitors at home
- ☐ wearing special holiday clothing
- ☐ watching Christmas specials on TV
- ☐ eating special foods
- ☐ seeing Santa
- ☐ having school vacation
- ☐ going to special church services
- ☐ singing Christmas songs and carols
- ☐ decorating for Christmas
- ☐ enjoying fun and excitement
- ☐ going to parties

The true meaning of Christmas, for me, is

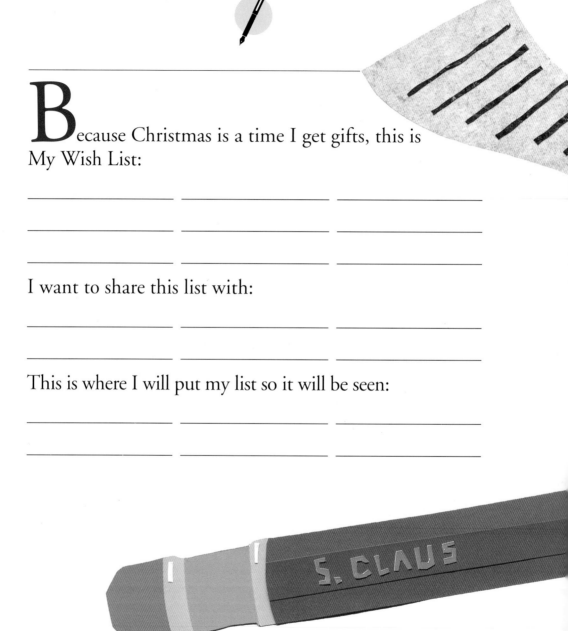

B
ecause Christmas is a time I get gifts, this is
My Wish List:

_____   _____   _____

_____   _____   _____

_____   _____   _____

I want to share this list with:

_____   _____   _____

_____   _____   _____

This is where I will put my list so it will be seen:

_____   _____   _____

_____   _____   _____

S. CLAUS

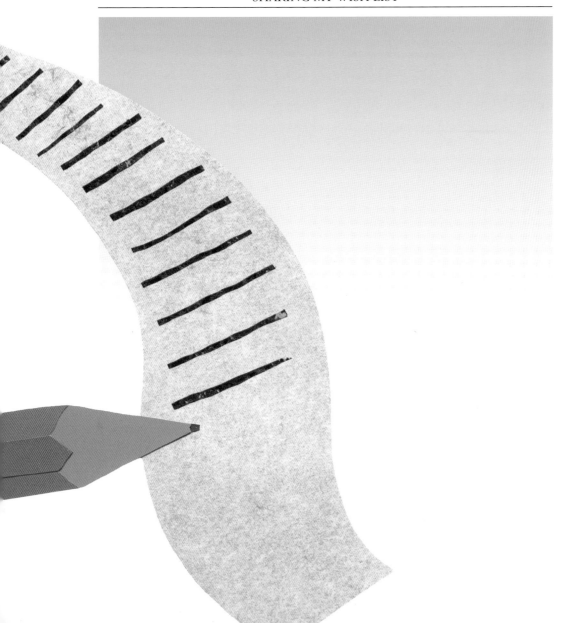

To

This is my Christmas gift list :

Name of person I'm giving a gift to	Gift ideas for this person
_____	_____
_____	_____
_____	_____
_____	_____

I will get these gifts by:
- ☐ shopping at a holiday fair
- ☐ buying them in stores
- ☐ making them at school
- ☐ making them by myself

My Christmas spending money comes from:

_____

(relatives, savings, working for it, gift money, etc.)

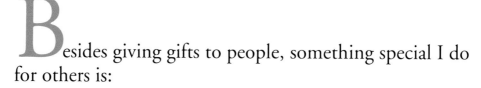

Besides giving gifts to people, something special I do for others is:

□ make visits to _____

□ donate food or toys to children at _____

□ do volunteer work at _____

□ help my family by _____

□ do a Christmas performance for _____

□ other _____

I do these things because _____

_____

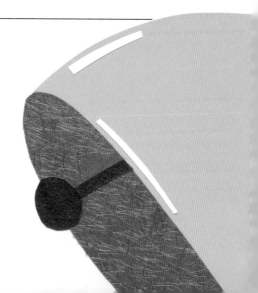

All the "Santa Claus" things that I do are:

☐ write letters to him
☐ visit him
☐ listen to stories about him
☐ watch TV specials about him
☐ tell stories about him
☐ draw pictures of him
☐ have a breakfast with him
☐ have my picture taken with him
☐ leave out cookies for him
☐ other _____

My favorite Santa story is _____

_____

_____

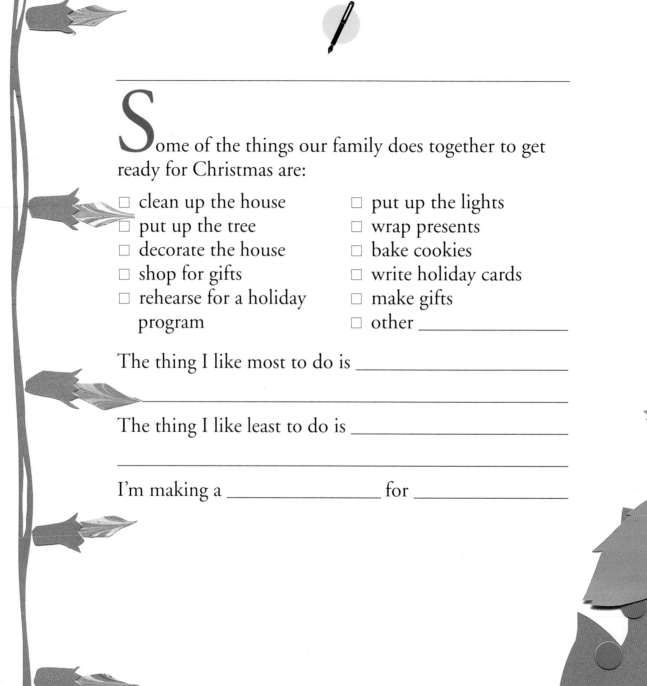

Some of the things our family does together to get ready for Christmas are:

- ☐ clean up the house
- ☐ put up the tree
- ☐ decorate the house
- ☐ shop for gifts
- ☐ rehearse for a holiday program
- ☐ put up the lights
- ☐ wrap presents
- ☐ bake cookies
- ☐ write holiday cards
- ☐ make gifts
- ☐ other _____

The thing I like most to do is _____

_____

The thing I like least to do is _____

_____

I'm making a _____ for _____

GETTING READY

22 23 24 25

Things I do to help count down the days until Christmas are:

☐ mark off the days on my calendar
☐ open a door each day on an Advent calendar
☐ get a special treat each day
☐ remind everyone about the number of days left
☐ other _____

In the weeks before Christmas I try to act _____

_____

My family says that I act _____

_____

2

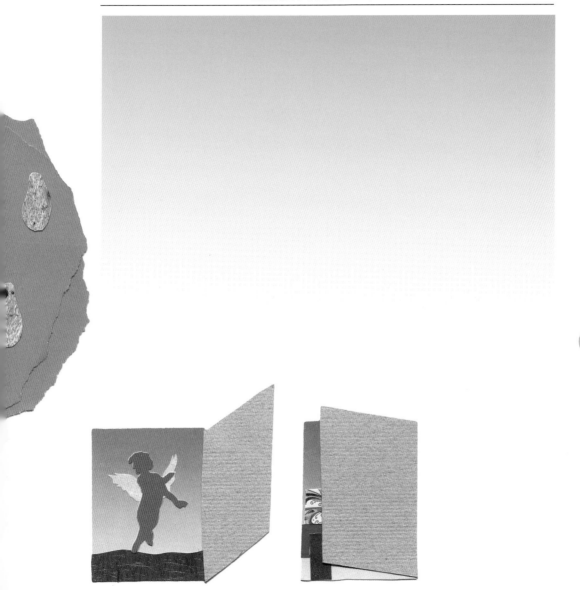

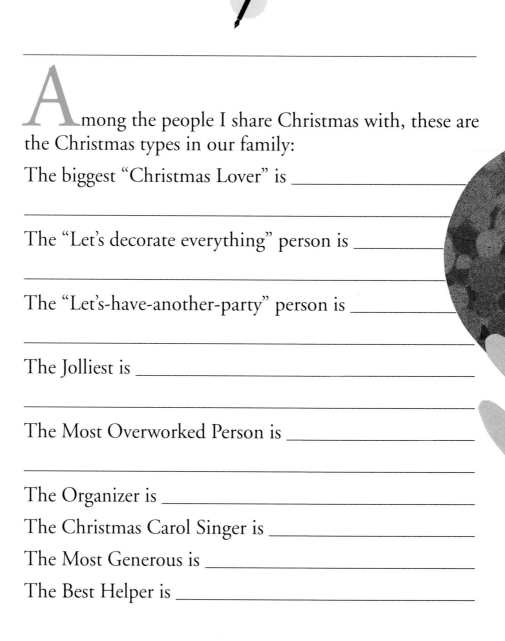

Among the people I share Christmas with, these are the Christmas types in our family:

The biggest "Christmas Lover" is _____

_____

The "Let's decorate everything" person is _____

_____

The "Let's-have-another-party" person is _____

_____

The Jolliest is _____

_____

The Most Overworked Person is _____

_____

The Organizer is _____

The Christmas Carol Singer is _____

The Most Generous is _____

The Best Helper is _____

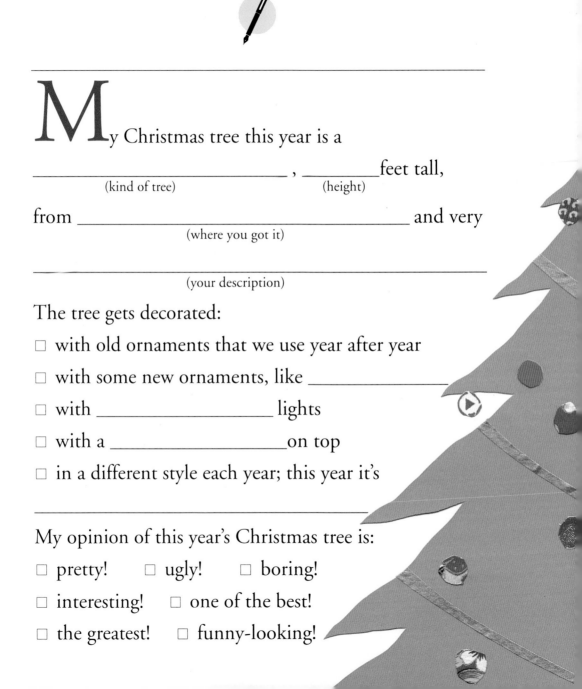

My Christmas tree this year is a

_____ , _____ feet tall,
　　　(kind of tree)　　　　　　(height)

from _____ and very

_____
(your description)

The tree gets decorated:

☐ with old ornaments that we use year after year

☐ with some new ornaments, like _____

☐ with _____ lights

☐ with a _____ on top

☐ in a different style each year; this year it's

_____

My opinion of this year's Christmas tree is:

☐ pretty!　　☐ ugly!　　☐ boring!

☐ interesting!　☐ one of the best!

☐ the greatest!　☐ funny-looking!

Traditionally, we celebrate Christmas Eve by :

_____

_____

Stockings are hung on _____

I go to sleep at _____

And dream about _____

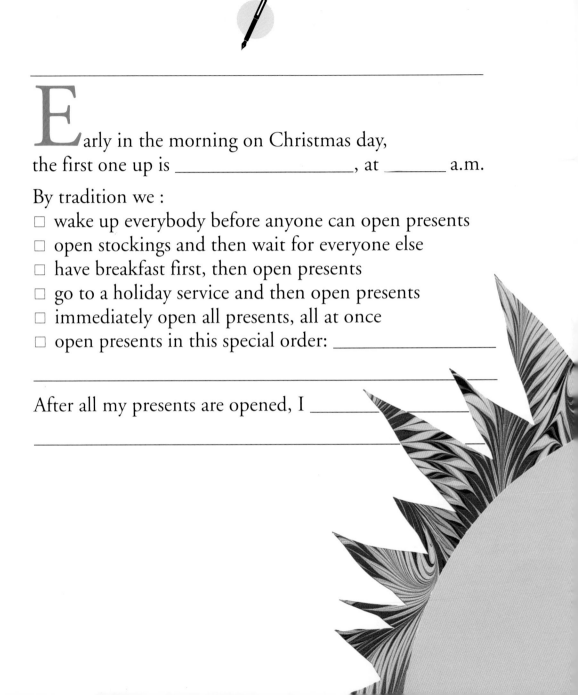

Early in the morning on Christmas day, the first one up is _____, at _____ a.m.

By tradition we :
- ☐ wake up everybody before anyone can open presents
- ☐ open stockings and then wait for everyone else
- ☐ have breakfast first, then open presents
- ☐ go to a holiday service and then open presents
- ☐ immediately open all presents, all at once
- ☐ open presents in this special order: _____

_____

After all my presents are opened, I _____

_____

CHRISTMAS MORNING

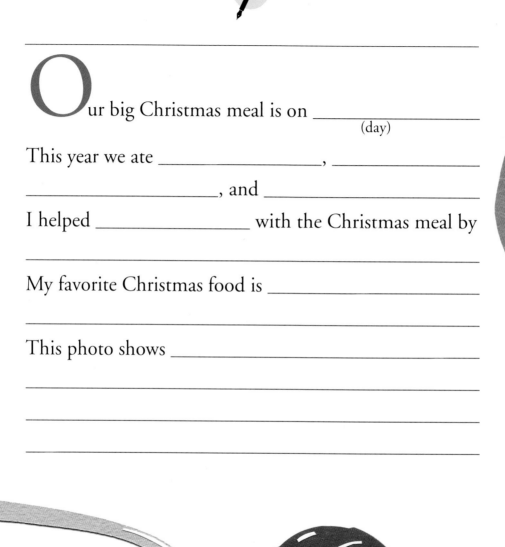

Our big Christmas meal is on _____
(day)

This year we ate _____, _____

_____, and _____

I helped _____ with the Christmas meal by

_____

My favorite Christmas food is _____

_____

This photo shows _____

_____

_____

_____

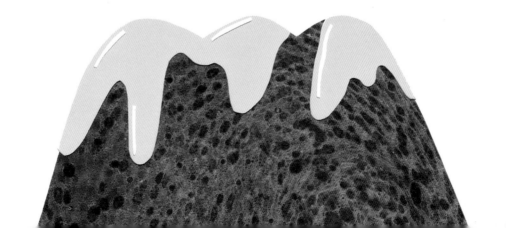

I sing Christmas songs _____

_____
(when, where)

My favorites are _____ _____

The funniest holiday song is _____

The one Christmas song I get tired of hearing so often is

_____

This photo shows _____

During the Christmas holiday: Number

The number of visitors to our house   _____

The number of places I visited   _____

The number of places I preferred not to visit   _____

The number of visiting kids who
wanted to play with my new presents   _____

The number of my friends who
came to show off their "new stuff"   _____

The number of visitors who slept overnight   _____

The number of hugs and kisses I got from
visitors and when I went visiting   _____

The number of holiday cookies I ate   _____

I think the Number 1 visitor was

After the big day (Christmas) was over, I spent the rest of my vacation:

☐ playing with my new presents

☐ just hanging around

☐ having friends over

☐ making visits

☐ working on _____

☐ traveling to _____

☐ staying over at _____'s house

☐ other _____

The best gift I received was _____

because _____

The one thing I wish I could have done on the Christmas

holiday was _____

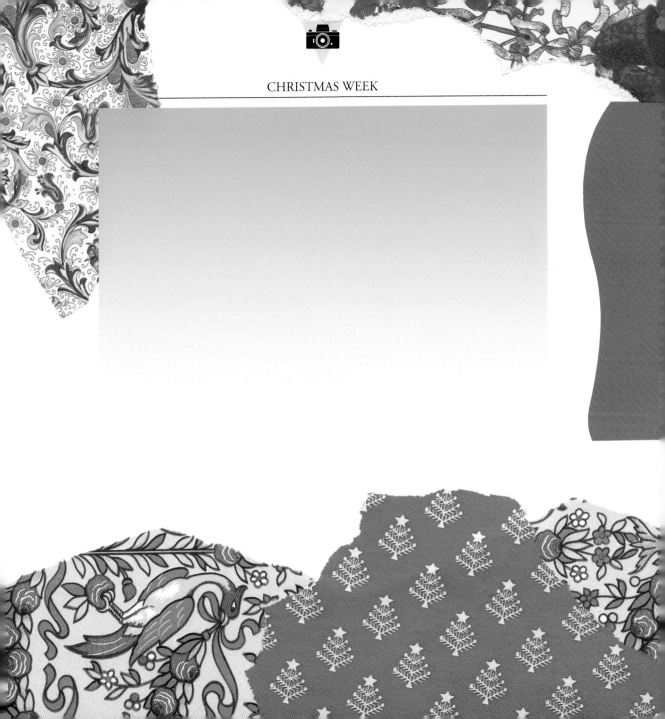

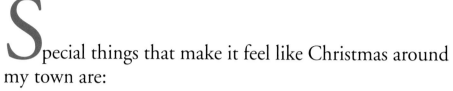

S pecial things that make it feel like Christmas around my town are:

The Christmas sights of _____

The Christmas smells of _____

The Christmas sounds of _____

The Christmas spirit of _____

Other _____

_____

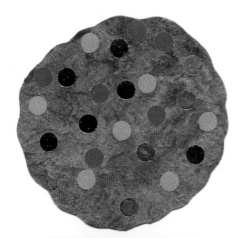

The concerts, parties, programs, pageants and church services that helped make this Christmas season so special were:

A concert at _____

A holiday program at _____

A Christmas pageant at _____

A church service for _____

My holiday party on _____

The holiday party I went to at _____

This photo shows _____

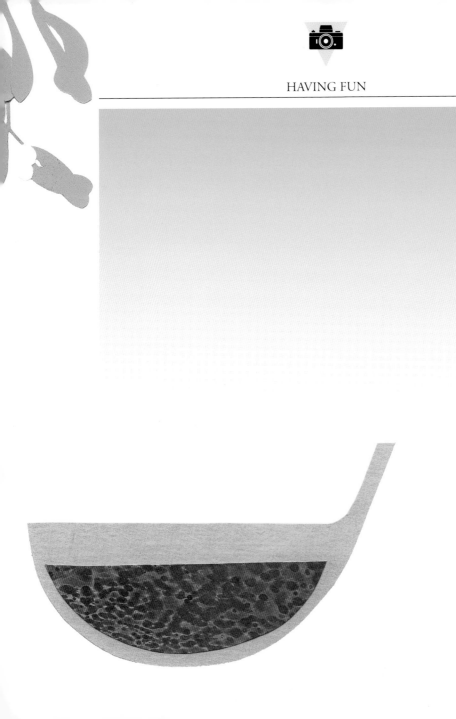

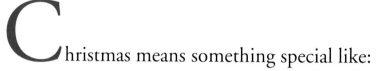

Christmas means something special like:

A hug from _____

A big kiss for _____

A cup of steamy _____

A snuggle under _____

A calm secure place like _____

A daydream of _____

A warm, cozy feeling when _____

_____

These are the holiday parties I attended:

_____   _____   _____

_____   _____   _____

_____   _____   _____
     (where)   (when)   (kind)

This is the party I gave: _____
                                  (kind)

Guests were _____

We ate _____

We did _____

We laughed at _____

We were surprised when _____

We ☐ exchanged ☐ did not exchange gifts/grab bag gift

_____

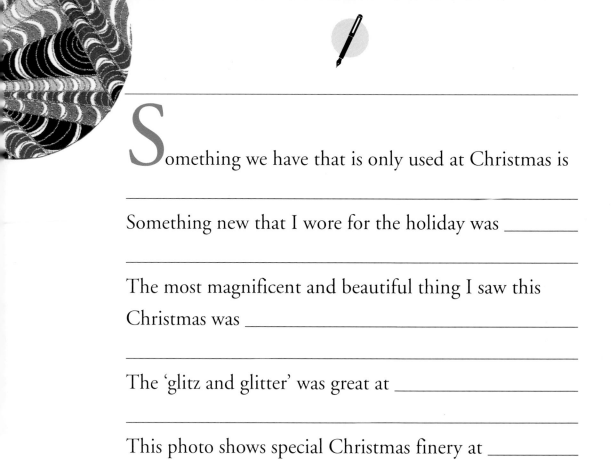

Something we have that is only used at Christmas is

_____

Something new that I wore for the holiday was _____

_____

The most magnificent and beautiful thing I saw this
Christmas was _____

_____

The 'glitz and glitter' was great at _____

_____

This photo shows special Christmas finery at _____

_____

SOMETHING SPECIAL

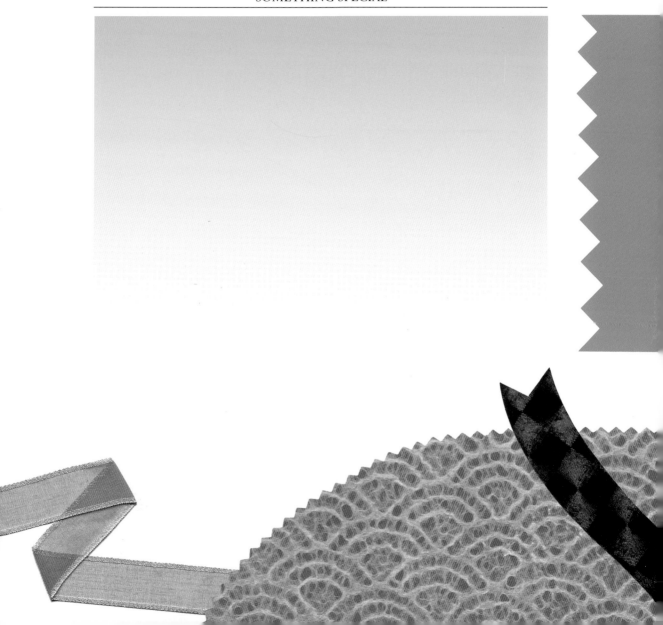

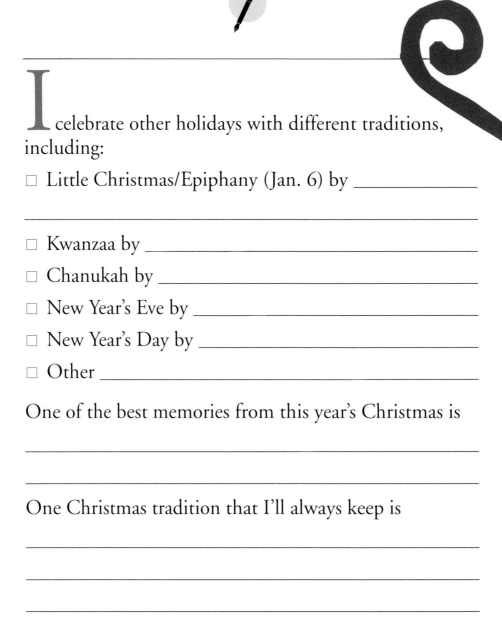

I celebrate other holidays with different traditions, including:

☐ Little Christmas/Epiphany (Jan. 6) by _____

_____

☐ Kwanzaa by _____

☐ Chanukah by _____

☐ New Year's Eve by _____

☐ New Year's Day by _____

☐ Other _____

One of the best memories from this year's Christmas is

_____

_____

One Christmas tradition that I'll always keep is

_____

_____

_____

CELEBRATING

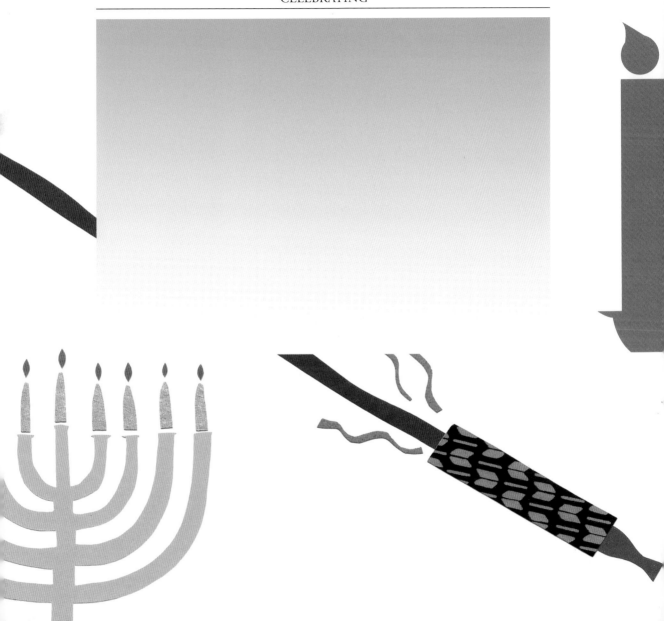

Design by Jenkins & Page, New York, NY.
Art Photography by Gamma One Conversions, New York, NY.
Composed in Adobe Garamond.
Type proofs by Impressive Prepress, New York, NY.
Printed and bound by Toppan Printing Company, Ltd., Singapore.